Sōl Chaos

Caitlin Salovich

BookLeaf Publishing

India | USA | UK

Presentation by *BookLeaf Publishing*

Web: www.bookleafpub.com

E-mail: info@bookleafpub.com

ISBN: 9789360941345

First edition 2024

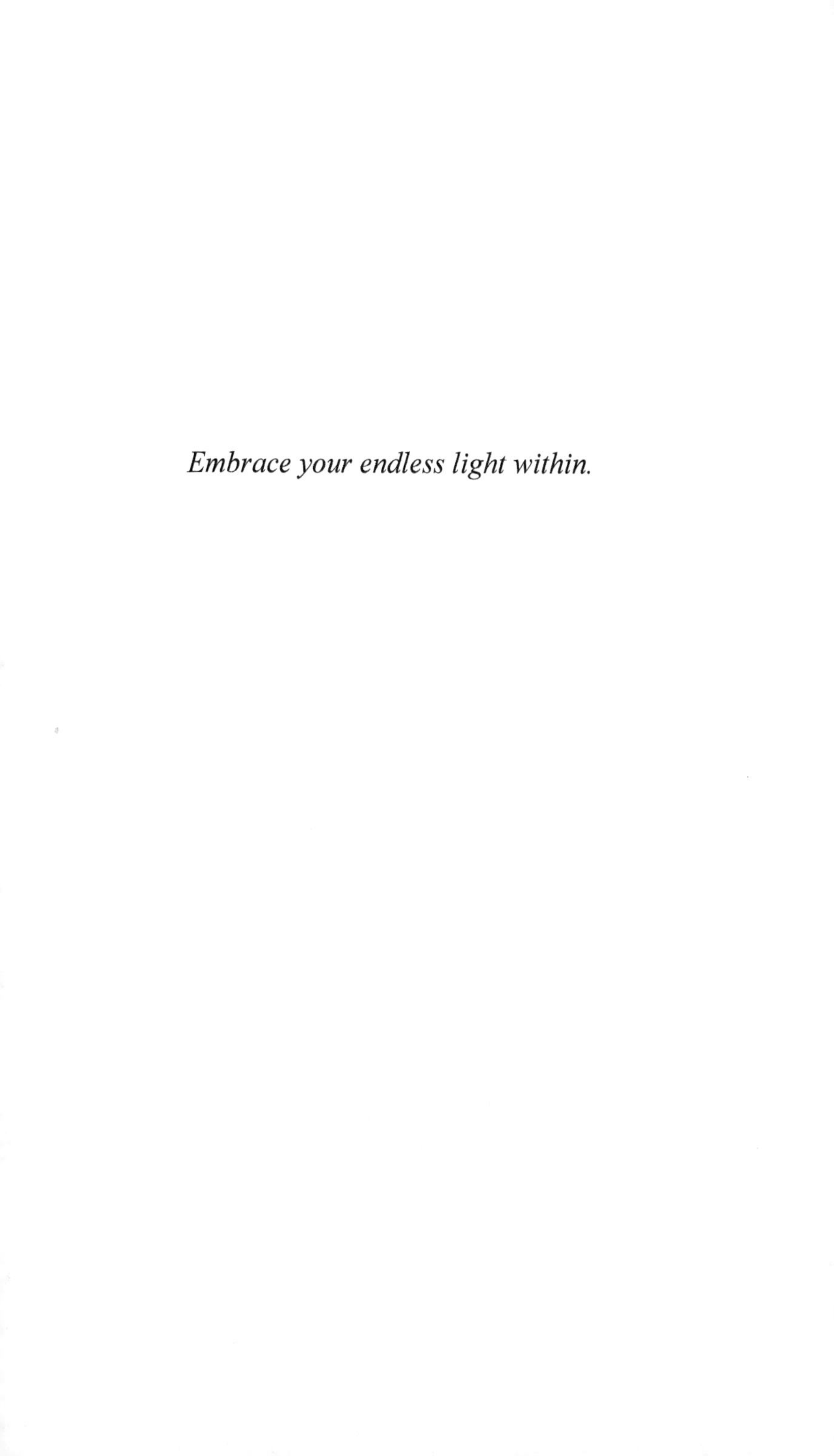

Embrace your endless light within.

ACKNOWLEDGEMENT

Infinite gratitude and appreciation have woven this collection into existence. To my readers, thank you for sharing in the solace and chaos that make up the poetic landscape of our neverending soul journey.

PREFACE

May these verses resonate with the universal cadence of the human spirit.

mōna

she possesses a certain essence

a captivating magnetic existence
birthing investigations to last every lifetime

a symbol of darkness or of light?

two avenues of healing
Self's inner most wounds

does she call you to perform under her beams
evoking a primal dance to rejuvenate and
cleanse?

what do her whispers speak?

allow her silence to soften your soul

can you feel her longing inquiry?

endless acknowledgment
of mystery beyond

all while simply glowing

rendezvous

crashed and burned
ashes seeking forgiveness

reconciled in flames
extinguishing aged parts still clinging to the
insufferable

a rare courage to accept this
venture of the unknown

wounds deeply rooted
intertwined in spirit
a master excavation mandatory

extracting negativity and ruin
left behind by all before

eventually rooted in the mind
hopelessness invited into the heart following

processing of shame
forgotten and buried deep within the living body

a complete renewal
soul cleansing invitation

relinquished

My Self no longer
requesting permission for authenticity

unapologetic for attributes of wholeness
deserving and accepted in all space

welcome to a life worth living

forces of nature

4

breathe fire by nightfall
inhale exhale
all life's beginnings;

solid and unshaken,
reclaiming all energy within

grief enclosed for an existence

never located
& always longed for

artist [not] starving

frantic mindwarp
bypassing signs
fickle scrolling
an unmeasurable search

universal patterns
lost before us
what trickery is life

pure entertainment
to real eyes
absolute intentional meaning

a discovery spread wildfire
creating nonexistent havoc

a simplistic solitude mastered

by words pouring out onto parchment

colors clinging to an infant canvas

sounds orchestrating synchronicity

creation and breakthroughs

artwork is
from an inside into

comparable the stars with effortless alignment
governing a midnight tapestry

advanced unique creation
engage and receive offerings aplenty

transformative artistry

a fountain of youthful

7

misplaced identity

stemming from lack of love

expecting from a child
to save adults from themselves

legacy

created to shatter
generational chains
and eradicate family trauma

& for cycles to be put to death

honor your story
with respect to your lineage

misión cumplida

sol renaissance

I am

Unwavering Darkness
Curiosity Beckoning
The Macabre

The unanswered questions scattered in the
depths of shadows

the melancholy depressive manic

deep toxic shroud of cluttered usefulness
the lucid recluse conforming

a reflection with limits of infinity

a cathartic combination of single Human Form

the lightness that illuminates
the notorious void

when all seems null
a long-awaited happening

absolute presence unavoidable

Magnificent
Misunderstood
Benelovent

under no circumstances manufactured

I am rarely me

no strings attached

I will attain absolute self
the moment I can remain
safe in all parts of me

exposed, raw, vulnerable

and yet still loved for all the wreckage and
beauty

lacuna

12

a man, so eager to discuss nothing -

a woman, so hell-bent on misunderstanding
everything -

for the sake of love

two lost languages.

sincerest apologies,

no translation provided

darling

it was never a fault
found in your ability to love correctly,
even connect

rather exposing wicked parasites
a disease of many infected spirits

that fed painstakingly upon
your accessible shining and brilliance

untamed hysteria

she rains earth worry
and crumbles mountains with disapproval
singing euphoria

goddess footsteps
revitalizing ancient land
a wise procreation formation

her dark whispers rattle
awakening the bleak skyline
careful attitude

a wicked fruitful smile reckless
atop the begging trees

starving for rage and deception
confusion and careful curiousity

roaring laugher
brave free flowing

aquamarine jealousy
nourishment for inhabitants

she is wild feminine

be gone

15

the shadow of you frequents me

often uninvited
yet always familiar

revealing glimmers

of our inconsistent love syndrome

errors

a velvet black skirt of stars, to picture

a star-studded skirt, velvet kissed
black dressed silhouette

celestial petticoat, black backdrop mesmerizing

painted in the sable night

a velvetier sky

lined with constellations

a raven velveteen

such bewitching noire

blackout atmosphere
delicate twilight

stellar eve

phoenix

17

broken wings and promises
you never taught me how to fly

awol

18

a war inside yourself
when you won't let go

of a rose-colored faded memory

dangerous, armed and lovesick

gustav klimt

19

common souls spend time
afraid of existence

death is my sole destination

pathways illustrated by destiny and
recommended by fate

thoughtfully chosen, a lovely arrival

willful journey of the heart
of death and life

encore

nobody desires
a sincere conversation with their shadow

yet, such a meeting is necessary
for higher consciousness

checkpoint

new lifetimes present opportunity
revise as intended
or meet yourself once more

every single moment presenting freewill
The Human Essence

forever available
to all versions of you
without judgement, loss or destruction

your simple choice

but to outlive eternity
confided in your stubbornness

a self-made persecution

optimistically,

soul is waiting
for its embrace

aloha

why do you
stay kept away

always

is it comfortable to reside
in the shadows

forever?

ever curious for the light
that perpetually calls your name?

fearful concerns of what may be

possibilities kept unimagined

unconvincing wishes
lay dormant in your dystopian dreamland

a passive way of life

childhood imprints

appetizer popcorn baskets
family favorite restaurant
The Ground Round

littlest pet shop adventures
and outdoor picnics
hidden away in amber mountains

the winter we went sledding
down the biggest hill
nearly frozen and comical

seasonal walmart hauls
and sunday reservations
tonight on disney's wonderful world

school breaks and magnified summers
nestled in the quiet
dreamland shenandoah valley

giggles blooming from a love-filled garden
observing neighbor birds and fancied butterflies

nature documentaries with grandad
a loving reminder of stillness

shared stories of childhood and wonder
told with an intriguing playfulness

these are reminiscing golden memories
livelong with you, mother

extended days morphed to lightning years

we board a train
that carries swift pace forwards
no empathy for the past
or for nostalgic travelers

you're so far gone now
And I am willfully able
to find you again

on occasion, I do
fondly lost in years passed
where I had you here still,

these were the days

www.ingramcontent.com/pod-product-compliance
Lightning Source LLC
La Vergne TN
LVHW021343200726
843509LV00014B/2648

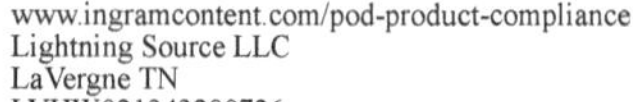